DISCOVER
ANIMAL LIFE

Contributing Writer
Lynne Hardie Baptista

Consultant
Mark Rosenthal

Publications International, Ltd.

ISBN: 0-7853-6108-1

Photo credits:
Front cover: **John Warden/SuperStock**
Back cover: **Getty Images**

Animals Animals: L.L.T. Rhodes: 14 (center); G.H. Thompson: 16 (bottom right); **Kent & Donna Dannen:** 30 (left), 37 (center); **©Educational Images Ltd., Elmira, NY, U.S.A. All rights reserved. Used by permission:** 24 (bottom); Ron West: 9 (center); **FPG International/Getty Images:** Age Fotostock: 37 (bottom); David Austen: 6 (bottom); C. Fitch: contents (right center); Michael S. Kass: 42 (bottom); Lee Kuhn: 26 (bottom), 28 (top), 39 (center); Richard Laird: 38 (bottom left); H. Lanks: 8 (bottom); Bill Loch: 24 (center); Stan Osolinski: 8 (center), 25 (bottom), 35; T. Quing: 43 (right center); Gary Randall: 18 (center), 22 (center), 39 (bottom), 42 (top & center); Scott Rea: 32 (center); Scott Roessler: 14 (bottom); Len Rue, Jr.: 20 (bottom); A. Schmidecker: front endsheet (top right), 29 (bottom left); Gail Shumway: title page, contents (bottom), 18 (top & bottom), 21 (top left & bottom left), 23 (top left & top center), 27, 34 (center), 43 (top right); J. Taposchaner: 38 (top); Telegraph Colour Library: front endsheet (bottom left), 21 (bottom right), back endsheet (right center); David Ward: back endsheet (bottom left); Larry West: 4 (bottom), 5, 8 (top center), 9 (bottom right), 10 (bottom); **Ray Gudas:** 39 (top); **Heather Angel Photography:** front endsheet (top left), 7 (bottom), 15 (top & center), 31 (left), 34 (top), back endsheet (top left); **Andrew Henley/Biofotos:** 40 (right); **Tom Stack & Associates:** 7 (left); Walt Anderson: 11 (bottom); John Cancalosi: 11 (center), 23 (bottom), 26 (top); Mary Clay: 20 (top); Gerald & Buff Corsi: 29 (top left); Chris Crowley: 7 (right); David M. Dennis: 4 (top), 6 (top), 10 (right center), 21 (top right); E.P.I. Nancy Adams: 16 (top left); Warren Garst: 40 (left); Dick George: 8 (top left); John Gerlach: 40 (bottom), back endsheet (bottom right); Kerry T. Givens: 10 (top); Thomas Kitchin: contents (top left), 15 (bottom), 17, 41 (top); Larry Lipsky: 12 (right); Joe McDonald: 30 (bottom); Gary Milburn: 16 (top right), 29 (bottom right), 30 (right), 36, 41 (left & right); Brian Parker: 4 (center), 13, 16 (bottom left), 19, 28 (bottom), 37 (top), 43 (top left & left center); Don & Ester Phillips: 8 (top right); Rod Planck: contents (top right); Milton Rand: 10 (left center); Kevin Schafer: contents (left center), 33 (top); Wendy Shattil/Bob Rozinski: front endsheet (left center & right center); John Shaw: 9 (top), 33 (bottom), 38 (center); Denise Tackett: 23 (top right); Larry Tackett: 24 (top), 34 (bottom); Roy Toft: 29 (top right); Greg Vaughn: 6 (center); **The Wildlife Collection:** Gary Bell: 12 (left), 14 (top); Ken Deitcher: 7 (center), 9 (bottom left); Michael Francis: 25 (top); John Giustina: 25 (center), 28 (center), 31 (top); Martin Harvey: front endsheet (bottom right), back endsheet (top right); Chris Huss: 22 (top & bottom); Tim Laman: 31 (right); Dean Lee: 33 (center); Clay Myers: 20 (center), 32 (bottom); Robert Parks: 11 (top); Jack Swenson: 32 (top); **Robert Winslow:** 38 (bottom right), back endsheet (left center).

Lynne Hardie Baptista is the author of *Discover Rain Forests* and numerous articles and award-winning education programs on wildlife conservation and the environment. Previously with the World Wildlife Fund, she is the director of education at the American Zoo and Aquarium Association.

Mark A. Rosenthal is the curator of mammals at the Lincoln Park Zoological Gardens. He has worldwide field experience and has contributed to several documentaries on zoological species management. A member of the American Society of Mammalogists and the International Primate Society, he has a master's degree in zoology from Northeastern Illinois University.

Illustrations: Lorie Robare

CONTENTS

INSECTS ARE EVERYWHERE.

You can find them on land, in the air, and in water. There are at least one million species of insects in the world, and many thousands of new species are discovered every year. Scientists believe several million more insect species have not yet been discovered!

We are all familiar with bees, ants, flies, spiders, crickets, cockroaches, and grasshoppers, but have you ever seen a walking stick or a rhinoceros beetle?

Insects are *invertebrates* (in-VER-tuh-brayts), which means they have no backbone. They belong to a large group of animals called *arthropods* (AR-throw-pods). Scorpions, spiders, ticks, mites, millipedes, crabs, and lobsters all belong to this group.

4

COCKROACHES AND TERMITES

Unwanted guests in our homes, schools, and workplaces, cockroaches are one of the oldest insect groups—dating well over 300 million years.

There are some 3,500 species of cockroaches and perhaps thousands more that scientists have not yet discovered.

They will eat almost anything, from soap and paper to birthday cake and dog food. Most cockroaches have flattened bodies that enable them to crawl into tiny cracks and crevices by night and to hide in drains and sewers by day.

Cockroaches are long-lived and produce large numbers of offspring. The common household pest, the American cockroach, can live more than four years and produce as many as 1,000 eggs!

Other cockroach species that invade our homes are the German cockroach and the Oriental cockroach. But not all species are pests. The Madagascar large hissing cockroach, for example, is kept as a pet by some people!

Termites happen to be related to cockroaches, and some species eat dead plant material, including wood, and some species can be very destructive. If not controlled, termites can destroy buildings.

Although termites are sometimes called white ants, they are not ants at all. In fact, ants are termites' deadliest enemies.

The termites' preference for dead plants is a benefit, because they return nutrients to the soil in a form that living plants can use.

Some termites build nests underground, while others build spectacular mounds that rise as high as 20 feet.

CRICKETS AND GRASSHOPPERS

On a typical summer night, you might hear the "chirp" of an American field cricket. You are hearing the male, singing to attract a potential mate. Crickets and grasshoppers are well known for their "songs," which they make in several ways. Some species rub together special veins on their wings. Others rub a bumpy hind leg against their wings.

Crickets, grasshoppers, locusts, and katydids (KAY-tee-didz) are all members of the same insect group. There are more than 20,000 different species, and they are found almost everywhere in the world, except for very cold places.

Crickets, grasshoppers, and locusts have evolved to live in numerous ways. Locusts live together in huge groups called "swarms." Desert locusts, for example, found in northern Africa and parts of Asia, swarm by the hundreds of millions. They migrate, or travel, across huge areas of land and eat millions of acres of crops in their path.

Other species live alone. To avoid predators, some of them have developed fascinating ways of hiding themselves from their enemies. The South American grasshopper looks exactly like a stick, blending well with its rain forest habitat. This makes it harder for predators to see them. A type of katydid that lives in Malaysia seems to disappear when it rests on the bark of a tree. This adaptation is known as *camouflage* (KAM-uh-flahj).

A cricket (left) has long feelers, or antennae, that wave continuously, picking up air currents. The antennae of a grasshopper (right) are much shorter.

These insects are known for their ability to jump long distances with their powerful hind legs.

Some katydids that live in the rain forest resemble bright green leaves.

Larger than the average grasshopper, the migratory locust travels in huge swarms that destroy farm crops and, in many countries, contribute to famine.

7

BEETLES

Among the better known beetles, ladybugs are beneficial to humans because they eat aphids (AY-fids), tiny bugs that destroy crops.

Beetles come in all shapes and sizes, but they all have one thing in common. What looks like a front pair of wings are not really wings at all. They are *elytra* (EL-uh-truh), tight-fitting sheaths that cover and protect the softer hind wings that are actually used for flying.

There are more kinds of beetles than any other type of insect— at least 300,000 species!

The dung beetle gets its nourishment from animal droppings, which it shapes into a ball and rolls into its burrow.

The word "scarab" is sometimes used to describe a stone or gem cut in the shape of the scarab beetle. Ancient Egyptians considered these insects a sign of good luck.

There is a wide variety of feeding habits among beetles. Some are predators and feed on other insects. Other beetles, like leaf beetles, eat plants.

Beetles have a great many adaptations to suit different needs, such as finding a mate or escaping enemies. Fireflies, which are beetles in spite of their name, have certain chemicals on the tips of their abdomens that glow at night. Male and female fireflies use these "lights" to communicate with each other. Many beetles taste bad or are poisonous, and they advertise this fact with bright, distinctive color patterns. If touched, the South African blister beetle will release a chemical that can burn the skin. Its bold black-and-white body warns predators to stay away. When disturbed, the click beetle makes loud clicking sounds to frighten off enemies.

8

FLIES

Blackflies, gnats, mosquitoes, and tsetse flies all belong to the same group of insects that are sometimes called two-winged flies. These insects are probably the most hated because of the terrible diseases they can spread to humans and livestock. Malaria, sleeping sickness, and a wide range of intestinal disorders are spread by these blood-sucking insects.

Unlike most other insects, two-winged flies have just one pair of short, strong wings. These wings allow them to fly very fast and even backward, to hover like a helicopter, and to land almost anywhere. Some species, like the common housefly, can land and even walk on ceilings!

Some flies are actually beneficial to humans. Certain species, like hover flies, are important pollinators of plants. Frequent visitors to our gardens, they move from flower to flower, accidentally spreading pollen as they feed.

Other species of flies are beneficial because they feed on dead animals or on animal droppings. This may sound disgusting, but it is an important service. Coffin flies and blowflies, for example, feed on dead animals. The waste material is digested by the fly and broken down into useful nutrients that are returned to the soil. These nutrients are then absorbed by plants through their roots.

The mouthparts of flies and mosquitoes are specially adapted for piercing through skin.

Most of us have been bitten by a housefly or a mosquito, but not all flies are pests.

Fruit flies are small but important because they help decompose vegetable matter by eating it.

Excellent mimics of bees, hover flies help keep predatory birds away!

Despite their unpopularity with humans, flies play a vital role in nature, pollinating flowers and recycling nutrients as they scavenge for food.

9

ANTS

Like termites, ants are highly social insects that live together in nests called colonies. Within the colonies, the worker ants maintain the nest, protect it from invaders, and provide food for the queen and the young ants, called *larvae* (LAR-vee).

There are at least 14,000 different kinds of ants, considered by many who study them to be among the most fascinating animals on Earth.

The carpenter ant is so named because of its preference for dead or decayed wood as a food source.

Leaf-cutting ants carry pieces of leaves to their underground nests, where they chew them up to make a kind of compost to fertilize the fungus they grow for food.

Most ant species are not as aggressive as army ants, which will attack any animal that happens to get in their way.

Ants display an incredible variety of habits and ways of living. All ants live in groups called colonies, but these may be located underground, in wood, or in tall mounds. Unlike other ant species, army ants have no permanent nest. Instead, they are always on the move in search of food, "marching" forward like soldiers in columns that

can be yards long. The colony moves rather slowly—at the rate of about one foot per minute.

Army ants feed mostly on other insects but they will attack any slow-moving animal in their path. Army ants usually pose no threat to humans because most people can get out of their way.

Some ants have developed unique relationships with plants or other insect species. The black garden ant lives with aphids and protects them from predators. In exchange, the aphids provide the ants with a special food called "honeydew." Honeydew is a sweet, sugary liquid that the aphids secrete after feeding on plants.

In Southeast Asia, certain plants provide a home for ants in exchange for food. These plants have hollow stems that make ideal nest sites for ants. The ants use some of the space as a "dump" where they store insect remains and other waste products. The plant will absorb the nutrients from the decomposing waste.

BEES AND WASPS

Bees and wasps are related to ants, but not all species are social. Certain kinds of hunting wasps are solitary predators. They seek other insects for food and kill them with a powerful stinger. Paper wasps, however, are highly social, living in an intricate nest made from wood fibers and saliva.

Bees are strict vegetarians. They collect pollen and nectar from flowers and are among the world's most important plant pollinators. Many bees rely on just one species of plant for food.

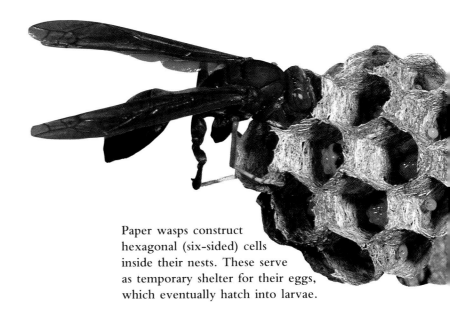

Paper wasps construct hexagonal (six-sided) cells inside their nests. These serve as temporary shelter for their eggs, which eventually hatch into larvae.

There are three kinds of honeybees. Each colony has one large queen bee, a number of slightly smaller males known as drones, and lots of much smaller worker bees, all of which are female. A big colony may have as many as 60,000 bees.

A colony can have only one queen. When an old queen sees worker bees building special cells that will produce new queens, she leaves the colony with as many bees as will follow her to start a new colony somewhere else.

If their hive is threatened by a predator, honeybees produce a chemical that signals all of the bees to attack. Honeybees have barbed stingers that usually remain in their victims. Most of the time, the bees die trying to free themselves.

A honeybee that has found food uses figure eights, circles, body-wagging, and loud buzzing to communicate its exact location to the other bees in the nest.

Not all bees have stingers, but even stingless bees inflict nasty bites. Some species can also release a stinging chemical.

Swarming occurs when a honeybee queen leads a large group of bees to start a new colony in another location.

LIFE IN THE SEA

began some 120 million years ago, when the first fish appeared. Scientists believe that these early *vertebrates* (VER-tuh-brayts)—so classified because they have backbones—are the ancestors of all land-based vertebrates, including amphibians, reptiles, birds, and mammals.

Today there are about 30,000 species of fish in the world, ranging in size from half-inch-long gobies to giant whale sharks that can reach a length of 70 feet. Of these, all but some 2,300 species are found in the ocean. The rest are found in fresh water.

Humans and fish have had a unique relationship for thousands of years. Besides being an important food source, fish are hunted for sport and collected as pets. The goldfish has been a member of Chinese households for more than 4,500 years!

CARTILAGINOUS FISH

The stingray is so named because of the spines that grow from its tail. The poison in them can be painful but will rarely kill a human.

Resembling sharks, sawfish are actually elongated rays. The largest can attain lengths of 20 feet or more.

Sharks are probably the most feared of all fish, but only a few of the 250 shark species truly pose a threat to humans.

The great white shark is the largest predatory fish. It can weigh as much as three tons, reaching lengths of 27 feet.

Sharks, rays, and skates are all cartilaginous (kar-ti-LAJ-in-us) fish, which means their skeletons are mostly or entirely made of cartilage, not bone.

Sharks are carnivorous (kar-NI-vor-us), feeding mainly on fish, crustaceans, and mollusks. The great white shark, tiger shark, blue shark, lemon shark, and large hammerhead shark are considered the most dangerous to humans.

Hammerhead sharks are perhaps the most unusual-looking of all sharks. There are 12 species of hammerheads, so named because their heads have hammerlike extensions on each side.

Skates and rays are flat, with winglike fins that make them look as though they are flying through the water like butterflies. Most species live on the bottom of the ocean, where they feed on oysters, snails, lobsters, crabs, and shrimp. Skates and rays usually live in cool ocean waters, but several species of South American stingrays live in fresh water.

Sawfish are also members of the cartilaginous group. Sawfish have a long, armored snout with sharp teeth on each side. The "saw" is used as a weapon. The sawfish will swim into a school of fish and slash its saw back and forth, killing or wounding as many fish as it can before settling down for a meal.

14

SALMON, TROUT, AND PIKE

Salmon belong to a group of fish that includes trout, pike, and pickerels. These fish are among the most important food fish in the world. They are also prized by sportfishing fans.

The fish spends the first few years of its life in fresh water, then travels out to sea. After several years in the Atlantic, it returns, swimming upstream, to the same river in which it was hatched. Salmon seem to stop at nothing to reach their destination, making tremendous leaps to clear obstacles in their way. Once they have reached their birth river, the salmon will lay eggs, or spawn.

Scientists believe that salmon can find their way back to these rivers by using memory and a sense of smell. Salmon remember the smell of the water, rocks, and vegetation of their birth river.

Trout are also very tasty, and certain species are popular game fish. Trout can be found both in the ocean and in fresh water, but most species prefer cold, fresh water. The rainbow trout is so named because of the colorful stripe on its flank. The brook trout is a popular sport fish because it puts up a good fight when hooked.

Pike and pickerels are solitary, aggressive fish that are found mostly in fresh water. These fish have large, pointed teeth and are efficient predators. Pike and pickerels are long, slender fish that have alligatorlike snouts.

The Atlantic salmon performs what is perhaps the most amazing migration in the animal world.

Salmon are powerful swimmers, but are hardly a match for hungry bears that gather along the rivers where the fish come to breed.

The rainbow trout is native to North America, but it has been introduced to many other parts of the world.

CATFISH

Catfish vary in size from the small varieties that are kept in aquariums to huge specimens that can weigh more than 250 pounds!

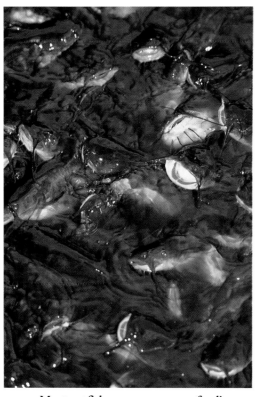

Most catfish are scavengers, feeding on animal and vegetable matter.

All catfish have at least one pair of whiskerlike extensions, called barbels, on the upper jaw. Some may also have a pair on the snout and additional pairs on the chin.

Because of its highly transparent body, the glass catfish is a popular aquarium fish.

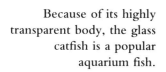

Most of the more than 2,000 species of catfish live in fresh water, with just two families found in warmer ocean waters.

Some species of catfish are quite unusual. Electric catfish can produce a strong electrical discharge with a force of up to 450 volts. These shocks are enough to kill small fish, which the catfish will eat, but it also uses these shocks as a powerful defensive weapon.

The Upside-down catfish of Africa actually swims on its back with its belly up! This allows the fish to grab food that is floating on the water's surface.

The Bronze catfish, originating in Trinidad, is one of the many types of catfish popular with hobbyists. Also popular is the glass catfish of Southeast Asia. This fish is almost completely transparent, and you can often see its internal organs! This is a special type of camouflage that enables the fish to almost completely disappear in the reflection of the water.

CICHLIDS

There are at least 600 species of cichlids (SICK-lids), most of them found in Central and South America, Africa, Madagascar, and parts of Asia. Nearly half of all cichlids are found in Africa, and most species live in freshwater streams and lakes.

Some cichlids are mouthbrooders. Either the male or the female holds the eggs in its mouth until they hatch. The young fish swim close to their parents' mouths and will often return there when danger threatens. Because of cichlids' unique behavioral patterns associated with reproduction, they are of great interest to many behavioral scientists.

Body shapes vary. Some are long and slim, while others are slightly round. Certain African species can weigh as much as 20 pounds. These larger species are important food fish. Some smaller varieties are very colorful and are kept in aquariums.

Some species of cichlids are vegetarians, while others are meat-eaters. As a result, cichlid mouths are quite varied.

Some species have blunt, chisellike teeth for cutting plants or scraping algae off rocks. Others have strong, pointed teeth for seizing and tearing prey. Still others have very small teeth, which they use to take the eggs or tiny newborn right out of parents' mouths!

Cichlids come in a great variety of colors and patterns.

Popular with hobbyists, the fish of this group tend to be aggressive, actively defending their territory.

As a group, cichlids eat almost every kind of food: water plants, plankton, small water creatures such as snails, and even other fish.

During breeding time, rival males challenge each other in their efforts to attract a mate.

17

AMPHIBIANS AND REPTILES

are quite different, but they are grouped together in the field of *herpetology* (her-pe-TAH-luh-jee). The word is derived from the Greek word *herpetos*, which means "creeping things."

Amphibians include frogs, salamanders, and wormlike *caecilians* (si-SIL-ee-uns). Best known among reptiles are turtles, lizards, snakes, and *crocodilians* (krah-kuh-DIL-ee-unz). All reptiles and amphibians are cold-

blooded creatures. They also have hearts that are alike in structure, but that's where the similarities end.

Scientists believe that the first amphibians evolved from fish. Eventually, they evolved into reptiles and, later, into birds and mammals.

18

CAECILIANS AND SALAMANDERS

Unlike reptiles, salamanders generally have moist skin. Like this barred tiger salamander, they are often boldly patterned.

Salamanders have slender bodies, long tails, and two pairs of legs that are about the same size.

Courtship behavior among salamanders takes many forms. Some species breed in water, others breed on land.

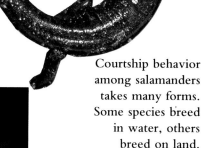

The bright color of this newt, a type of salamander, tells predators that it would not make a good meal.

Caecilians are long, limbless amphibians that look very much like earthworms. There are 164 species, found in Southeast Asia, Africa, and Latin America. Herpetologists know little about these secretive creatures, which spend most of their time burrowing beneath soil or on the floor of a body of water.

Caecilians are very diverse in size—ranging from the *Idiocranium* of West Africa, which measures about four and a half inches long, to the *Caecilia thompsoni* of Columbia, which is more than four feet long. Caecilians eat a wide variety of prey, from worms and termites to small lizards. Because most species are almost blind, scientists think they find food by smelling it.

Many people mistake salamanders for lizards. Salamanders live in cool, shady habitats in mild climate zones. They are usually active at night, and unlike their noisy relatives, frogs and toads, salamanders are also usually very quiet. During the day, salamanders rest under layers of dead leaves or under rocks in creeks to avoid the heat of the sun. At night, they hunt for worms, insects, and other prey.

Salamanders have a variety of lifestyles. Some, like the cave salamander, live entirely on land. Others, like the so-called water dog (also known as a mudpuppy), live in rivers or streams. Most newts, on the other hand, divide their time between land and water.

FROGS AND TOADS

Many people wonder what the difference is between frogs and toads. Toads usually have short legs, plump bodies, and rough or warty skin. They generally live on land and cannot jump as well as frogs. Frogs have more slender bodies, with long limbs and smooth skin, and they usually live near water.

At certain times of the year, you can hear a chorus of frogs calling to each other throughout the night. They do this by inflating one or more of the vocal sacs in their throats with air. Some of the species that you may have heard are the spring peeper, cricket frog, chorus frog, and American bullfrog.

During mating season, male frogs (left) call attention to themselves by making loud croaking sounds. With a body that is almost transparent, the glass frog (below) of Central America is an expert at going unnoticed.

All frogs and toads have at least a trace of poison that is produced in special glands in their skin. Most of the time this poison is not very strong. But the tiny poison-arrow frogs of Central and South America produce one of the strongest poisons in nature. In small amounts, the poison is not dangerous to large animals or humans, but many rain forest Indians put the poison from these frogs on the tips of their arrows.

Frogs and toads are the most numerous of all amphibians. There are at least 2,600 species, found throughout the world.

With their deep voices and heavy bodies, bullfrogs are more aggressive than other frog species. Males will kick and bite each other to establish control over a piece of territory.

21

TURTLES

Turtles may be slow, but some are pretty good travelers. The green sea turtle will migrate from the coast of Brazil to reproduce on the Island of Ascension in the Atlantic Ocean—a distance of 1,400 miles!

Today there are about 250 species of turtles and tortoises. These reptiles are found in tropical and temperate regions on every continent except Antarctica.

Some turtles, such as sea turtles and softshell turtles, spend almost all of their lives in oceans, lakes, or rivers. Bog turtles and wood turtles live in wetland habitats. Tortoises, a term used to refer to a specific group of turtles, live only on land. But wherever they live, all turtles lay their eggs on land.

The turtle's unique feature is its protective shell. A turtle shell has about 60 bones and is made up of two parts—the *carapace* (KAR-uh-pace), which covers the turtle's back, and the *plastron* (PLAS-trun), which covers its belly. Most species can pull their legs and heads inside their shells when a predator appears.

Turtles first appeared on Earth about 200 million years ago, long before the dinosaurs. They have changed very little over the years.

There are six species of sea turtles, but all are very rare because people have killed too many of them. Hawksbill sea turtles, for example, were hunted for their beautiful shells. These were made into jewelry, souvenirs, and eyeglass frames. Others, such as the green sea turtle, were killed for their meat and skin. Today, all sea turtles are protected by law, but some are still killed illegally.

Turtles can live very long lives. American box turtles have been known to reach ages of more than 100 years.

The Galapagos tortoise, a protected species, has suffered because people have introduced rats, dogs, and other "foreign" animals to its island home.

Turtles do not have teeth. They use their beaklike snouts to rip and cut their food. As a group, turtles eat an amazing variety of foods—from insects and fruit to jellyfish and worms.

LIZARDS

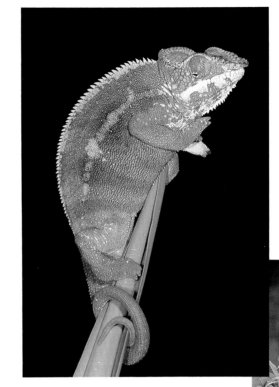

Chameleons have *prehensile* (pre-HEN-sil) tails, meaning that their movement can be controlled, allowing the animals to wrap them around tree limbs for extra stability.

Lizard movement is fascinating to observe, as many species have adapted unique ways to get around. Geckos (GE-koze), for instance, have many ridges on the bottoms of their feet, which help make them excellent climbers.

Chameleons (kuh-MEE-lee-uns) also are excellent climbers, moving slowly through trees in search of insect prey. These lizards have *zygodactyl* (zy-guh-DAK-tul) feet. This means that some toes face forward and some face backward.

Some lizards are excellent swimmers. The Bornean earless lizard uses snakelike movements to propel its body on both water and land.

Lizards have adapted a wide range of defenses. The horned toads of North America have sharp spines on their heads and bodies, and most predators avoid them. Chisel-teeth lizards and chameleons use camouflage to avoid being seen. Some lizards play dead when attacked. Predators that are stimulated by movement will lose interest in prey that seems lifeless.

Numbering some 3,000 species, lizards are probably the most diverse of all reptiles.

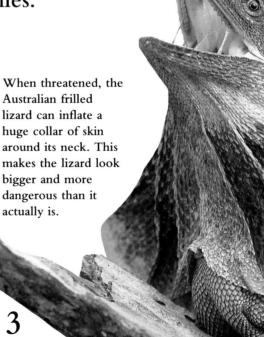

The komodo dragon, the largest of all monitor lizards, can reach a length of 10 feet and weigh more than 350 pounds.

When threatened, the Australian frilled lizard can inflate a huge collar of skin around its neck. This makes the lizard look bigger and more dangerous than it actually is.

23

SNAKES

With a jaw that can "unhinge," many snakes can eat prey that is much larger than their own heads.

The body of a snake is covered with a scaly skin, which helps it move along the ground. Snakes shed their skins several times a year.

There are at least 2,500 varieties of snakes in the world. Despite the fact that these reptiles have no legs, many species, like the American racer, are extremely swift. Most snakes move by flexing their bodies in a series of S-shaped curves, using plants, rocks, or rough ground as push-off points.

This same movement is used by water snakes and garter snakes, which spend most of their time in water, to swim. Snakes that live in trees, like American tree boas, vary this S-shaped movement. These snakes slither through the trees with accordion-type maneuvers, using their prehensile tails for a better grip.

Snakes are carnivores, feeding on insects, birds, worms, mammals, fish, lizards, and even other snakes. Food is swallowed whole, because snake teeth are designed for catching and holding prey, not for chewing.

Some snakes, such as pit vipers, have heat sensors on their faces that help locate the direction and distance of prey, even in complete darkness.

Some species, like boas, pythons, and rat snakes, dispatch their prey by *constriction* (kun-STRIK-shun), which means they wrap themselves around their victim and squeeze until it suffocates.

Others, like rattlesnakes and coral snakes, are poisonous, killing their victims with deadly venom. Poison enters a victim's body through the snakes' fangs.

Snakes can detect prey with their eyes, but also by using their tongues. When snakes flick their forked tongues in and out of their mouths, they pick up chemical signals.

It is not difficult to imagine how the rainbow boa, found in Central and South America, got its name. The rainbow boa and the other 59 species of boas are not dangerous to humans.

CROCODILIANS

There are 22 species of reptiles known as crocodilians. The list includes alligators, crocodiles, and gavials (GAY-vee-ulz). These fascinating reptiles have changed little in the last 65 million years.

All crocodilians live near water in warm regions around the world. They have adapted special features that suit their watery lifestyles: webbed feet that help them swim and also walk on mud or sand; eyes and nostrils set high on their heads so they can see and breathe while being almost completely submerged; a third eyelid that protects their eyes underwater; and a strong tail that propels them through the water.

Crocodilians are powerful meat-eaters and will devour any animal they can catch. Strong, tooth-filled jaws tear and rip apart prey.

The gavial, also known as gharial (GER-ee-ul), is native to India. It gets its name from the potlike shape at the end of the male's snout. *Ghara* is the Hindi word for "pot."

Today, many crocodilians are rare because too many were killed for their beautiful skins. Crocodile and alligator hides have long been used to make shoes, purses, and other leather goods. Laws now protect most crocodilians. As a result, many species, including the American alligator, are making a comeback.

The American alligator belongs to the same family as the crocodile, but is typically heavier and less active. Alligators also have rounded snouts. Crocodile snouts are pointed and narrow.

A gavial (right) can grow to a length of 20 feet. Its main food is fish, but it will also eat frogs, birds, and other small animals.

Crocodilians spend most of their day basking in the sun, but become active at night in their search for a meal.

Alligators may attack deer and other large animals that come near the water.

Winged Creatures

are some of nature's most delightful animals. Think how different our lives would be without the gentle song of the nightingale or the simple beauty of the cardinal.

All birds, whether they fly or not, have wings. The peregrine (PER-uh-grin) falcon, the world's fastest flier, has long, pointed wings. Birds that live in forests, such as the great horned owl, have short, broad wings. Even flightless birds, like the penguin, rely on their wings. Shaped like flippers, they help the bird dive and swim.

There are about 8,600 species of birds worldwide. These warm-blooded vertebrates have adapted themselves to live in almost any habitat—from the cold, windswept Arctic to the hottest deserts.

26

HERONS

Herons are long-legged, long-billed birds that spend all of their time near the water, even though they never swim.

Like some species of heron, the common egret was almost wiped out by feather hunters in the early 1900s. Today, it is found worldwide.

The great blue heron stands four feet tall and has a wingspan of around six feet. It makes a honking sound similar to that of a Canadian goose.

Herons (HEER-unz) and their relatives, bitterns (BI-ternz) and egrets (EE-grets), are found all over the world, primarily in wetland habitats.

Different species have different methods of locating prey—usually fish, insects, frogs, or worms. The black heron wades into shallow water and opens its wings, creating a shadow. It is not clear whether the fish mistake the shadow for shelter and swim toward it, or whether the shadow simply helps the heron see the fish better, but the system works.

The purple heron rarely wades into the water. It prefers to perch on reeds or low branches, waiting quietly for prey to appear.

Other species, such as the great blue heron, wade deep into the water, using their feet to stir up fish and other creatures hiding in the mud. Once the prey has been located, the heron will use its long bill to stab it with deadly accuracy.

Herons have beautiful feathers in shades of smoky white, light gray, and blue. Early in the 20th century, millions of herons were killed for their feathers, which were used to decorate women's hats. Large numbers of herons were wiped out, and many species became rare. Today, laws protect herons and their relatives from this senseless slaughter.

The tricolored heron is found in the marshes, lakes, and lagoons of the southeastern United States.

VULTURES AND CONDORS

With their bald heads and the slightly rumpled feathers that are common to some species, vultures are certainly not as beautiful as their more noble relatives, eagles and hawks. But vultures are important because they feed on dead animals, helping to keep habitats clean.

In Africa, the Griffon vulture and the Cape vulture follow the migration of large animals like the wildebeest (WIL-de-beest) and zebra. With their long, broad wings, these birds can soar in the sky for hours.

The king vulture (left), found in Central and South America, is the most colorful of all vultures.

With a wingspan of nine feet, the California condor is North America's greatest soaring bird. Through captive breeding, over 50 birds survive in the wild.

Another type of vulture, the Andean condor of South America, is also a *scavenger* (SKA-ven-jer). With a wingspan of up to ten feet, it is one of the world's largest birds.

Almost as large is the California condor. Overhunting and pesticide poisoning nearly wiped out this species. Today, there are only about 75 California condors in existence—the majority of them in captivity.

Vultures belong to a group of birds that includes falcons, eagles, and hawks, otherwise known as birds of prey, or *raptors* (RAP-terz).

Vultures generally have keen eyesight, powerful beaks for tearing flesh, and bald heads that can be thrust into an animal's body without fouling any feathers.

TURKEYS

Some domestic turkeys have white feathers, but most are black and bronze.

Smaller than the common turkey, this Central American species has never been domesticated.

When you hear the word "turkey," you probably think of the chubby gobbler that graces your holiday dinner table. This domestic turkey is a descendant of the common turkey, which is native to North and Central America. Domestic turkeys can be more than three times heavier than their wild relatives, sometimes weighing in at 60 pounds or more! The domestic turkey is completely dependent on humans and cannot survive in the wild.

The common turkey is a much more streamlined bird. It lives in open woodland and forest clearings, where it

feeds on seeds, berries, and small reptiles such as salamanders and lizards. Turkeys have bare heads and necks, as well as large throat patches called *wattles* (WA-tulz). Males also have sharp horns on each leg called *spurs*. When a male is seeking a mate, he puts on a fancy courtship display. Strutting back and forth, he rattles his wing feathers, swells his wattle, opens his tail feathers, and gobbles loudly.

Female turkeys build nests by themselves, laying 8 to 15 eggs. Sometimes female turkeys will share a nest, so they can better protect their eggs.

Turkeys are game birds and are popular targets for hunters. Not good fliers, they prefer walking instead of taking to the air.

Europeans had never seen turkeys until Spanish explorers brought them home from Mexico during the 16th century.

Wild turkeys prefer wooded areas near water. Their diet consists of seeds, berries, nuts, insects, and an occasional frog or lizard.

COCKATOOS

Found mainly in Australia and New Guinea, cockatoos are members of the parrot family.

Cockatoos have sharp, sawlike beaks that are used to open seeds and fruits. In fact, the name "cockatoo" is derived from the Malayan word *kakatua,* which means "pincers." Like other parrots, cockatoos can use their hooked bills as a third foot to climb trees or to grasp food. Some varieties have cheek patches that change color—to red or blue, depending on the species—when they are alarmed.

Cockatoos have large crests on the tops of their heads. These normally lay flat, but are raised when the bird is excited. The sulfur-crested cockatoo's bright yellow crest stands out nicely against its white body. Not all cockatoos are white, however. The great black cockatoo has grayish-black feathers and crimson cheek patches, while the gang-gang cockatoo is usually a grayish color.

Cockatoos spend most of their lives in trees, occasionally coming to the ground to feed. Like most perching birds, their claws are structured to give them a strong grip on tree branches. Cockatoos have a most unusual way of keeping clean. They bathe themselves by flying among wet leaves or by hanging upside down during rain showers.

Like most cockatoo species, the Moluccan cockatoo is mostly white in color.

They are popular as pets, but too many have been taken from the wild. Today, many varieties are rare.

The sulfur-crested cockatoo has a tuft of yellow feathers atop its head that the bird can fan open at will.

The palm cockatoo, also known as the great black cockatoo, is the largest of the 17 species in this bird group.

31

SANDPIPERS

Different species of sandpipers will flock together in huge numbers of up to 100,000 birds.

Numbering 80 different species, sandpipers are the most common shorebirds in the world.

Sandpipers gather at sea beaches and inland mud flats to search for food.

During the winter, the western sandpiper looks almost identical to the semipalmated sandpiper.

Sandpipers are found throughout the northern parts of both Europe and North America. Most species are migratory. They breed in wetlands or grasslands and winter along coastal areas.

Most sandpipers prefer open country near water, where they feed on snails, clams, shrimp, aquatic worms and insects, and sometimes, plants. At low tide they feed together in the shallow mud and sand.

When the tide comes in, these wading birds retreat to high salt marshes or nearby farmland. In the morning, when the tide goes back down, the birds return to the shore to feed once again.

Most sandpipers are a spotted brown or gray, with pale or white feathers on their underparts. The feathers of some species change color with the seasons. All species have long wings and short tails, though many have pointed, falconlike wings that enable them to fly very fast.

Across the species, sandpipers have a variety of bill types because of the different ways they gather food. The curlew sandpiper, for example, has a large curved bill that it uses to probe for snails, clams, and other sea creatures, while the broad-billed sandpiper has a heavy bill that allows it to feed on larger prey.

PUFFINS

Short-winged birds with heavy bodies, puffins are found in the northern extremes of North America, Europe, and Asia. They are part of a group of some 22 species of seabirds known as auks (AWKS).

Sometimes called sea parrots, puffins have large parrotlike bills that are brightly colored in shades of orange, yellow, and blue. This gives puffins an almost comical appearance, particularly during the summer breeding season when their bills become larger and brighter. When the season is over, the outer layers of the bills are shed—not unlike a deer shedding its antlers—and they return to their original size.

In one respect, at least, puffins are unlike parrots. They are silent birds, although they can make a deep growl.

Puffins can fly, but they are somewhat awkward in the air. Puffins are at their best in the water, where they use their wings as flippers to dive and swim in search of fish.

The birds live in large groups called colonies during the summer months. When fall arrives, they leave their breeding grounds to spend the next nine months at sea.

Puffins raise just one chick each year. Every day for the first six weeks after a chick hatches, one of its parents flies out to sea, returning to the nest with a bill full of small fish.

Puffins are similar to penguins in many ways, but the two species aren't even distantly related.

The Atlantic puffin (above) can carry as many as ten fish at a time, holding them crosswise in its beak. The tufted puffin (right) grows yellow plumes along the sides of its head during the summer breeding season.

The horned puffin is a Pacific relative of the common (or Atlantic) puffin.

WHAT IS A MAMMAL?

The playful river otter, the odd echidna (e-KID-nuh), and the magnificent African elephant look very different at first glance, but they all belong to this unique category of animals. Did you know that *we* also belong to this group?

There are more than 4,000 kinds of mammals in the world, and all share certain characteristics. Mammals are warm-blooded vertebrates. Skin covers their bodies, but unlike other animals, mammals also have hair.

Mammal skin also contains many kinds of glands. Some glands produce sweat, while others produce the oil that helps lubricate fur. The glands that make a mammal a mammal, however, are the mammary glands. These glands produce milk that female mammals use to nurse their young.

34

PRIMATES

Like most lemurs, the mongoose lemur has large eyes and a somewhat doglike face.

Primates range in size from the tiny mouse lemur, which weighs only 2 ounces, to the gorilla, which can weigh 600 pounds.

What do you have in common with a chimpanzee, a mountain gorilla, and a spider monkey? You are all closely related mammals—you are primates (PRY-mayts).

As you might have already guessed, there is a wide diversity among primates, but there are some traits that all share. Most primates have "opposable thumbs," which means that their thumbs can rotate to touch the fingertips on the same hand. This helps primates climb trees and grasp food. Also, primates can see in color, and their brains are generally larger than those of other mammals.

The more primitive primates, called *prosimians* (pro-SIM-ee-unz), include the strange aye-aye, lemurs (LEE-merz), and the sifakas (si-FAH-kuz). These tree-dwelling primates live on the island of Madagascar. Galagos (guh-LAY-goze), lorises (LOR-i-sez), pottos (PAH-toze), and tarsiers (TAR-see-erz) are also prosimians. Scientists believe that the earliest primates that appeared on Earth some 70 million years ago were similar to some of the mammals in this group.

The pygmy marmoset (right) is only about six inches long, but it is an excellent tree climber. The long, white "moustache" of the Emperor tamarin (below) gives it a comical look.

The "higher" primates include marmosets (MAR-moh-sets), tamarins (TAM-uh-rinz), monkeys, apes, and humans. Found only in South America, marmosets and tamarins are squirrel-sized primates that are some of nature's most spectacular mammals.

Marmosets and tamarins eat fruit, flowers, nectar, insects, frogs, and spiders. They live in close family groups of between four and 15 individuals. All members of the group help raise the young—sharing food and even carrying them from time to time. It's possible that these "babysitters" are learning how to care for the offspring that they will have one day.

Most primates do not exhibit this kind of family cooperation, but some do live in smaller family groups made up of a male and female and their immature offspring. Gibbons and their cousins, the siamang (SEE-uh-mang) monkeys, live in groups such as this. In titi (ti-TEE) monkey family groups, the male takes the lead role in caring for the young. He is the one who is in charge of feeding, protecting, and carrying the infant until it is about four or five months old and mature enough to keep up with its family.

The great apes—chimpanzees, orangutans, and gorillas—are human beings' closest relatives. These amazing animals have many behaviors and physical characteristics that are just like ours. Apes have no tails, and they have long arms and highly developed brains. Gorillas are usually described as being of either the lowland or mountain variety. The mountain gorilla is an endangered species. Only a few hundred remain in the mountains of East Africa.

The orangutan (left) is among the apes most clearly related to human beings. Despite its ferocious reputation, the gorilla (below) is for the most part a peaceful animal.

Scientists have been able to teach chimpanzees and gorillas words by using sign language.

Intelligent, sociable animals, chimpanzees communicate with each other using a variety of sounds and facial expressions.

CARNIVORES

Raccoons make their homes in the hollows of large trees. There are only two species: the common raccoon shown here and the larger, crab-eating raccoon of South America.

There are about 230 species of carnivores, and these are some of the best known mammals in the world. Cats, dogs, bears, raccoons, weasels, and hyenas are all carnivores. Most mammals in this group are well-equipped for their meaty diets. They have long, pointed canine teeth and powerful jaws.

Carnivores have different ways of hunting. Some, like wolves and hyenas, hunt in groups called packs. Tigers, jaguars, and other cat species usually hunt alone. Once caught, prey is usually killed with a bite to the neck. Mongooses and weasels bite the backs of their victims' heads, and African wild dogs will aim for their prey's soft underparts.

Meat-eaters are at the top of the food chain and help keep nature's balance. Predators help keep the populations of their prey from growing too large. When hunting, predators often seek the weakest, oldest, or slowest victim, because these are usually the easiest to catch. In this way, carnivores help "weed out" unhealthy individuals.

Some carnivores have a mixed diet. The giant panda, an endangered species found only in China, feeds mainly on bamboo, but it will also eat bulbs, insects, and rodents. Raccoons, found throughout North and South America, will eat almost anything—from frogs to fruit. Many live near urban areas, and their nighttime raids on garbage cans can become terribly annoying.

Although some people think that carnivores are cruel killers, they play an important role in the balance of nature.

Wolves will eat most small animals and birds, but their main prey is deer, including moose and caribou.

When angered, the giant panda (above) will hiss and spit like a cat. The lion (right) has a deep voice capable of amazingly powerful roars.

HOOFED MAMMALS AND ELEPHANTS

Sheep, zebras, camels, and deer all belong to a group of mammals called *ungulates* (UN-gyoo-layts)—mammals with hooves. There are about 200 species of ungulates. Classified as even-toed ungulates are pigs and peccaries (PE-kuh-reez), giraffes, antelopes, and hippopotamuses. Odd-toed ungulates include rhinoceroses, horses, and tapirs (TAY-pirz).

Ungulates are usually *herbivores* (ER-bi-vorz), feeding on leaves, flowers, fruits, and grasses. Many species of ungulates live in large groups called herds. Most ungulates have an excellent sense of smell and large eyes on the sides of their heads.

Elephants, known as "primitive ungulates," are related to this large group of mammals. There are two species—the Asian elephant and the African elephant.

Unfortunately, both elephant species have suffered great losses over the years. Although they are protected by law, both species are losing their habitats to an ever-increasing human population.

Elephants live in close family groups that are led by the oldest females. All members of the herd help raise the young elephants, which rely on adult care until they are 12 to 13 years old. When male elephants reach this age, they leave the group, preferring to live alone or in all-male herds.

Elephants are the largest land animals in the world (adult males can reach weights of 16,000 pounds!), and many people consider them the most magnificent. Unfortunately, many have been killed for their ivory tusks.

There are some 200 species of hoofed animals. The list includes pigs, horses, giraffes, antelopes, and hippopotamuses.

Even when they are only a few days old, young sheep, called kids, can go almost anywhere their mothers lead them.

Giraffes may look awkward, but when frightened or attacked, they can run faster than any horse.

39

RODENTS AND RABBITS

Related to the guinea pig, capybaras (left) are found in the swamps and riverside forests of eastern and northern South America.

Rabbits are cute, but they can be pests. They breed quickly, and they will eat almost any growing plant.

Rodents are best known for the long, chisellike front teeth that stick out of their upper jaws. These teeth never stop growing. They must be ground down every day with a good chewing on a piece of wood.

Rodents range in size from the tiny harvest mouse to the capybara (ka-pee-BAR-uh)—an aquatic rodent that looks like a guinea pig but can weigh more than 100 pounds! Scientists classify rodents into three main groups, based on the structure of their jaw muscles. The first group includes chipmunks, squirrels, and beavers. Rats and mouselike rodents make up the second group. The third group includes porcupines and guinea pigs.

Although they look like rodents, scientists have grouped rabbits and hares separately because of differences in their teeth and skeletons. There are about 45 species of rabbits and hares. All have long ears and hind legs, furry bodies, and fluffy, upturned tails. Hunted by many different animals—including humans—they can run very fast when threatened.

Pikas (PIE-kuz) are closely related to rabbits and hares. Fourteen species of pikas live in North America, Eastern Europe, and Asia. These lively creatures spend most of their summer and fall days collecting grasses and drying them in the sun. Later, they will store this hay and use it as winter food.

There are about 1,700 species of rodents in the world. Nearly 40 percent of all mammals belong to this group.

Squirrels are found all over the world, except Australia and the polar regions.

40

BATS

Bats range in size from the tiny Kitti's hog-nosed bat, with a wingspan of just six inches, to the huge Samoan flying fox, which has a wingspan of almost six feet! They live on every continent except Antarctica, feeding on everything from fruit and insects to nectar and, in some cases, blood. They have a remarkable ability to make the most of their habitats.

Bats are not blind. In fact, some have excellent vision. All bats depend on a unique system, called *echolocation* (e-koh-loh-KAY-shun), to navigate around obstacles, locate safe places to land, and find food in the dark. Echolocation works something like a submarine's sonar. Bats make high-pitched clicking sounds that bounce off nearby objects and are returned to the bats' ears as echoes. The echoes help the bats determine the location of prey and also help them avoid flying into branches or wires.

Bats are not the evil monsters that some people think they are. Many bats, especially those that live in the tropics, spread seeds and pollinate plants. Bats also eat mosquitoes and other insect pests. Some bats may snatch as many as 600 insects out of the air in just one hour!

Bats are the only mammals that have wings and can truly fly. With almost 1,000 different species, they comprise nearly one quarter of all existing mammals.

Bats usually rest during the day, hanging upside down by their toes in a cave or other dark place.

Fruit-eating bats (left) are found only in warm regions, where fruit is available year-round. There are only three species of vampire bats (below), but none are found in the United States.

41

WHALES AND DOLPHINS

The killer whale is the only member of the whale family that eats warm-blooded animals, particularly penguins and seals.

Mistakenly thought of as fish, cetaceans are actually mammals that have adapted to life in the water.

Because of its friendliness and apparent intelligence, the dolphin has fascinated humans since ancient times.

Unusual-looking beluga whales, also known as white whales, are found in the Arctic region and adjacent seas.

Some mammals have adapted completely to life in water. These mammals are called *cetaceans* (se-TAY-shuns). This group of sea mammals includes whales, dolphins, and porpoises. There are 92 species of cetaceans swimming in the oceans throughout the world.

The largest animal ever to live on Earth—the blue whale—still exists today. Not even the biggest dinosaur that ever lived grew as large as this gentle giant, which can measure 80 feet or more in length and weigh as much as 150 tons! To help stay warm in chilly waters, cetaceans have a layer of fat, called blubber, just beneath their skin.

Cetaceans are highly intelligent mammals, and many species have evolved complex ways to communicate with each other. Scientists are still trying to determine the meaning of the high-pitched squeaks of the humpback whale.

Like other mammals, cetaceans breathe air and must come to the water's surface to do so. They take in and release air through one or two blowholes on the tops of their heads. Some species, such as the sperm whale, can go for long periods of time without taking a breath. Sperm whales have been clocked underwater for over an hour without coming up for air!

NATURE'S ODDS AND ENDS

Shrews, moles, hedgehogs, and the strange-looking tenrec (TEN-rek) of Madagascar all belong to the group of mammals known as *insectivores* (in-SEK-ti-vorz). These mammals eat insects, but many also eat fish, frogs, mice, plant material, and even *carrion* (KER-ee-un), a polite term for rotting flesh. Insectivores are some of the most primitive of all mammals—and also some of the most unusual.

Another interesting group of mammals is the *edentates* (ee-DEN-tayts)—anteaters, sloths, and armadillos. Edentate means "without teeth," but only the anteater is truly toothless. Anteaters eat mostly ants and termites, using their long, sticky tongues to pull the insects out of their nests. Sloths, slow-moving mammals that spend their lives high in the tropical forests of Latin America, feed on plant material.

Kangaroos are probably the most famous of the *marsupials* (mar-SOO-pee-ulz), the group of mammals with pouches. There are actually some 260 marsupial species, including wallabies (WALL-uh-beez), American opossums (uh-PAH-sumz), wombats (WAHM-bats), and the koala (koh-AH-luh). A marsupial baby develops in a very unusual way. Just after its birth, the tiny, blind baby crawls from the birth opening to the mother's pouch. There it develops and grows, feeding on its mother's milk for ten months or more before it is ready to stand on its own.

The moment it is touched or hears a loud noise, the hedgehog (above) rolls itself into a ball. An opossum (right) may respond by pretending to be dead.

Mammals classified as insectivores, edentates, and marsupials are among nature's most unusual animals.

The koala (above) is a very picky eater, preferring the leaves of only a few types of eucalyptus trees. Kangaroos (right) have a more varied diet, which includes grass, grain, leaves, twigs, and fruit.

GLOSSARY

Amphibian (am-FIB-ee-un): An animal adapted to live both on land and in water.

Arthropod (AR-throw-pod): A group of animals that have external skeletons, jointed legs, and bodies divided into segments. Insects, spiders, and lobsters are arthropods.

Camouflage (KAM-uh-flahj): A way of blending into the surroundings to hide from predators or prey.

Carnivore (KAR-ni-vor): An animal that eats meat. Lions and eagles are examples of carnivores.

Cartilage (KAR-tuh-lij): A strong, flexible material that forms parts of the bodies of humans and other animals. A human nose is mostly made of cartilage.

Cold-blooded: Term used to describe an animal that is not able to maintain a constant body temperature. Amphibians, fish, insects, and reptiles are cold-blooded animals.

Endangered species: A plant or animal that is in danger of becoming extinct.

Extinct (ex-TINKT): Gone forever; wiped out. Dinosaurs and the dodo bird are extinct.

Food chain: A process in nature in which food energy is transferred from one living thing to another. An example of a food chain is a plant-eating deer that is eaten by a wolf.

Habitat: A specific area where an animal or plant lives and finds water, nutrients, shelter, and living space.

Herbivore (ER-bi-vor): An animal that eats plants. Deer and elephants are herbivores.

Herpetology (her-pe-TAH-luh-jee): The scientific study of reptiles and amphibians.

Incubate (ING-kyoo-bayt): To sit on eggs so as to hatch them using the warmth of the body.

Insectivore (in-SEK-ti-vor): An animal that depends on insects as food.

Invertebrate (in-VER-tuh-brayt): An animal without a backbone. Insects are invertebrates.

Larva (LAR-vuh): The newly hatched, wormlike form of some insects. A caterpillar is the larva of a butterfly.

Mammal (MAM-ul): The term used to describe warm-blooded higher vertebrates that have hair and nourish their young with milk produced by mammary glands.

Marsupials (mar-SOO-pee-ulz): Mammals such as kangaroos, wombats, and oppossums whose offspring are temporarily carried in a pouch on their mother's stomach.

Mimicry (MI-mi-kree): A type of camouflage in which a plant or animal looks like something else. Species use mimicry to hide from predators or prey, or to make themselves look dangerous or poisonous.

Omnivore (AHM-ni-vor): An animal that eats a wide range of foods, from plants to meat to carrion. Bears and raccoons are examples of omnivores.

Plankton (PLANK-tun): Tiny floating plants and animals that drift in the ocean and form the basis of many food chains.

Predator (PRED-uh-tor): An animal that hunts, kills, and feeds on other animals.

Prehensile (pre-HEN-sil): Designed to grab or hold onto things. Sea horses and chameleons have prehensile tails.

Primates (PRY-mayts): Any of the order of mammals that includes humans, apes, monkeys, and related forms, such as lemurs and tarsiers.

Scavenger (SKA-ven-jer): An animal that feeds on dead animals or trash. Vultures are scavengers.

Species (SPEE-sheez): A group of animals and plants that are closely related.

Vertebrate (VER-tuh-brayt): An animal with a backbone. Fish, birds, amphibians, reptiles, and mammals are all vertebrates.

Warm-blooded: Term used to describe an animal that is able to maintain a constant body temperature on its own. Birds and mammals are warm-blooded animals.